'Wake,
butterfl

MATSUO BASHŌ

Born 1644, near Ueno, Japan
Died 1694, Osaka, Japan

This selection taken from *On Love and Barley: Haiku of Bashō*,
translated with an introduction by Lucien Stryk and
published in 1985.

MATSUO BASHŌ IN PENGUIN CLASSICS
On Love and Barley
The Narrow Road to the Deep North and Other Travel Sketches

MATSUO BASHŌ

Lips too chilled

Translated by
Lucien Stryk

PENGUIN BOOKS

PENGUIN CLASSICS

UK | USA | Canada | Ireland | Australia
India | New Zealand | South Africa

Penguin Books is part of the Penguin Random House group of companies
whose addresses can be found at global.penguinrandomhouse.com.

Penguin
Random House
UK

This selection published in Penguin Classics 2015
002

Copyright © Lucien Stryk, 1985

The moral right of the translator has been asserted

Set in 10/14.5 pt Baskerville 10 Pro
Typeset by Jouve (UK), Milton Keynes
Printed in Great Britain by Clays Ltd, St Ives plc

A CIP catalogue record for this book is available from the British Library

ISBN: 978-0-141-39845-7

www.greenpenguin.co.uk

MIX
Paper from
responsible sources
FSC® C018179

Penguin Random House is committed to a
sustainable future for our business, our readers
and our planet. This book is made from Forest
Stewardship Council® certified paper.

In my new robe
this morning –
someone else.

Fields, mountains
of Hubaku, in
nine days – spring.

Year by year,
the monkey's mask
reveals the monkey.

New Year – the Basho-Tosei
hermitage
a-buzz with haiku.

New Year –
feeling broody
from late autumn.

Spring come – New Year's
gourd stuffed, five quarts
of last year's rice.

Matsuo Bashō

Plunging hoofs stir
Futami sand – divine white
horse greets New Year.

Spring night,
cherry-
blossom dawn.

Wearing straw cloaks,
with spring
saints greet each other.

Spring's exodus –
birds shriek,
fish eyes blink tears.

Matsuo Bashō

Ploughing the field
for cherry-hemp –
storm echoes.

Spring rain –
under trees
a crystal stream.

Monks' feet clomping
through icy dark,
drawing sweet water.

Spring moon –
flower face
in mist.

Spring rain –
they rouse me,
old sluggard.

Ebb tide –
willows
dip to mud.

Sparrows in eaves,
mice in ceiling –
celestial music.

Dark night –
plover crying
for its nest.

Matsuo Bashō

Over skylark's song
Noh cry
of pheasant.

How terrible
the pheasant's call –
snake-eater.

Hozo mountain-pass
soars
higher than the skylark.

Bush-warbler dots
the rice-ball
drying on the porch.

Bucking the oven
gap – cat
yowls in heat.

Now cat's done
mewing, bedroom's
touched by moonlight.

Do not forget the plum,
blooming
in the thicket.

Spring air –
woven moon
and plum scent.

Mountain path –
sun rising
through plum scent.

Another haiku?
Yet more cherry blossoms –
not my face.

Sleeping willow –
soul of
the nightingale.

Behind the virgins'
quarters,
one blossoming plum.

Matsuo Bashō

First cherry
budding
by peach blossoms.

Red plum blossoms:
where behind the
bead-screen's love?

Pretending to drink
sake from my fan,
sprinkled with cherry petals.

If I'd the knack
I'd sing like
cherry flakes falling.

Matsuo Bashō

Striding ten, twelve
miles in search of
cherry wreaths – how glorious.

Under the cherry –
blossom soup,
blossom salad.

Reeling with *sake*
and cherry blossoms,
a sworded woman in *haori*.

Boozy on blossoms –
dark rice,
white *sake*.

Come out, bat –
birds, earth itself
hauled off by flowers.

Waterfall garlands –
tell
that to revellers.

Spraying in wind,
through blossoms,
waves of Lake Grebe.

Be careful where
you aim,
peaches of Fushimi.

Matsuo Bashō

Sparrows
in rape-field,
blossom-viewing.

Cold white azalea –
lone nun
under thatched roof.

Draining the *sake*
cask – behold,
a gallon flower-vase.

On my knees, hugging
roots, I grieve
for Priest Tando.

Matsuo Bashō

Taros sprouting
at the gate,
young creepers.

Search carefully –
in the hedge,
a shepherd's purse.

Aged – eating
laver, my teeth
grind sand.

Cherry blossoms –
lights
of years past.

Matsuo Bashō

Squalls shake the Basho
tree – all
night my basin echoes rain.

On the dead limb
squats a crow –
autumn night.

Kiyotaki river –
pine needles wildfire
on the crest.

Parting,
straw-clutching
for support.

Yellow rose petals
thunder –
a waterfall.

Whiter than stones
of Stone Mountain –
autumn wind.

Sparrow, spare
the horsefly
dallying in flowers.

Drizzly June –
long hair, face
sickly white.

Nara's Buddhas,
one by one –
essence of asters.

Darkening waves –
cry of wild ducks,
faintly white.

Faceless – bones
scattered in the field,
wind cuts my flesh.

Where cuckoo
vanishes –
an island.

Winter downpour –
even the monkey
needs a raincoat.

June clouds,
at ease on
Arashiyama peak.

Butterfly –
wings curve into
white poppy.

Summer wraps –
is there no end
to lice?

First winter rain –
I plod on,
Traveller, my name.

How quiet –
locust-shrill
pierces rock.

Wild mallow fringing
the wood,
plucked by my horse.

Futami friends, farewell –
clam torn from shell,
I follow autumn.

Matsuo Bashō

Traveller sleeps –
a sick wild duck reels
through cold night.

When I bend low
enough, purseweed
beneath my fence.

Poet grieving over shivering
monkeys, what of this child
cast out in autumn wind?

Poor boy – leaves
moon-viewing
for rice-grinding.

Wake, butterfly –
it's late, we've miles
to go together.

Violets –
how precious on
a mountain path.

Gulping June
rains, swollen
Mogami river.

Early autumn –
rice field, ocean,
one green.

Bright moon: I
stroll around the pond –
hey, dawn has come.

Storming over
Lake Nio, whirlwinds
of cherry blossoms.

From moon-wreathed
bamboo grove,
cuckoo song.

Visiting tombs,
white-hairs bow
over canes.

Skylark on moor –
sweet song
of non-attachment.

Clouds –
a chance to dodge
moon-viewing.

Birth of art –
song of rice planters,
chorus from nowhere.

Cresting Lake Omi's
seven misted views,
Miidera's bells.

Matsuo Bashō

Over Benkei's temple,
flashing Yoshitune's
sword – May carp.

Cormorant fishing:
how stirring,
how saddening.

Skylark sings all
day, and day
not long enough.

Year's end –
still in straw hat
and sandals.

Moonlit plum tree –
wait,
spring will come.

Snowy morning –
one crow
after another.

Come, see real
flowers
of this painful world.

Morning-glory –
it, too,
turns from me.

Travel-weary,
I seek lodging –
ah, wisteria.

Come, let's go
snow-viewing
till we're buried.

Chrysanthemum
silence – monk
sips his morning tea.

Crow's
abandoned nest,
a plum tree.

Matsuo Bashō

Melon
in morning dew,
mud-fresh.

Wintry day,
on my horse
a frozen shadow.

Summer moon –
clapping hands,
I herald dawn.

Drenched bush-clover,
passers-by –
both beautiful.

Harsh sound –
hail spattering
my traveller's hat.

Lips too chilled
for prattle –
autumn wind.

Not one traveller
braves this road –
autumn night.

Withered grass,
under piling
heat-waves.

Phew –
dace-guts scent
waterweed.

June rain,
hollyhocks turning
where sun should be.

Journey's end –
still alive, this
autumn evening.

How cold –
leek tips
washed white.

Matsuo Bashō

Firefly-viewing –
drunken steersman,
drunken boat.

Dewy shoulders
of my paper robe –
heat-waves.